EVENING TRAIN

EVENING TRAIN

TOM CLARK

B L A Z E V O X [B O O K S]
Buffalo, New York

publisher of weird little books

BlazeVOX [books]

blazevox.org

BlazeVOX

Acknowledgements:

Some of these poems first appeared in *Poetry* magazine, as well as in the Bunchgrass Press limited edition chapbook anthologies *Myth, Official Leagues, For Hours Now, Envoy,* and on the *Tom Clark/Beyond the Pale* blog.

Contents

EVENING TRAIN

Moving House

We were always moving out
ahead of the next wave yet not
riding the last wave to the crest

history refracts the burden
and it all breaks back and down
and returns yet not the same, tipping

ill fitting puzzle bits of myth
captured and released
in transition to dust from real life

as time flows on away beneath
the ground
all the endless summer night long

Evening Train

Train whistle in cold January night
down by the water
lonesome sound
from a long way off
amid memory forest
Harlem Avenue 1947
or 1948
late
upstairs
in the exile bedroom
at grandparents' house
across from the house
of the mysterious famous gangster

in the dark
under the attic rafters
hour after hour
imagining a meaning
to fit
the brilliant silvery word
Zephyr

Taking the El to Work

I make it out the door to the El station.
It's a hot summer day in 1955.
Heat waves jump off the El tracks.
From the train you can see down into the backyards
Where angels live in dejection.
Ragged wash hangs there: grey t-shirts without arms.
Next come vistas of wrecked cars and the bolt factory.
Downtown I change trains for the North Side
Or the South Side. One night late
I'm walking down 35th Street toward the El
When out of the double doors of a bar
Explodes a woman screaming as if escaped
From hell, her torso a red streaming suture.
I decide I am unsuited for this line of work
But the next night I'm back on the train to the ballpark.

Pancake and Pizza Breakfast

Yellow Olds with 1970 Iowa plates so bilious you put me in mind
   of adventure
seeking back in the lost time
when all it took to inspire the heart with a prolonged rush of
   expectation
was the idea of a deranged weekend at the Dells

Nice Surprise

There toward the end of that last Millennium, with only about sixty more years to go, when things were finally beginning to become just that little bit clearer, it was thought time to provide the child a soft, loyal, companionable stuffed friend.

But by then, it was perhaps too late.

The mask had slipped just enough to reveal the inchoate fear encroaching. What was it, merely a passing shadow, there, behind the child's untrusting eyes. That which had been suspected yet not thus far seen would indeed soon enough become actual, as incipient things have a way of doing.

First it's stuffed bunnies they're giving you. Next it's ice cream and then the nice surprise — you're at the hospital, having an operation.

The Past

There is no such thing
as a clean break
with the past

Chase it off, it comes sneaking
straight back
much as a blindly loyal

companion, whose
company one had never quite earned
and does not wish to keep

Point and Shoot

A wee bit
of intelligent
direction —

all reality
that hopelessly
awkward

and ungainly
proposal
forever spilling

over
into uncertainty
seemed

to need.

Words

Even in the middle of nowhere
there are words

words turn a nowhere into a putative somewhere

Like the arena exhortation at sports events to *CHEER!*
still flashing in the dark long after the partisans have departed

Styx

Getting away with it's the easy part
But what comes later, the flight
Into incompatible identities
Taking shadows hostage
On the descent...

Sliver

So is it the thin
sliver of light, slicing
through the curtain
from the window
of the person confined
in the equally dark house
next door
            that puts
the dread
of the lid
being closed
over one
into the mind
without a word
being said
across the slender divide

narrowing alley
crack of brightness between
still
solid masses
of trees, converging
overhead must be
even darker down there
in the shadows someone
absent
who wanted to speak

Nightly Encounter

so little time left now
and the double that walks beside
this vague luminous figure
materializing from night vapors
is a prisoner of memory

Castaway

casting the pain, the regret, the fear, the anger
away, as though
they belonged to a stranger
watching from the windblown shore
a distant sinking ship

Reflection

The surface of the pond remembers
Ripples of your reflection, rotting leaves;

In the stagnant past,
Your future weighs like a sunken stone.

Summer comes and goes, unnoticed
By the grunge flamingos wading in the turbid water.

Nebulous

Nebulous first quarter moon soap chip floating motherly
over the Bay
cradling a soft long cloud
and two young deer now half grown
and out at night alone
in search of a drink in the driest year
pause and gaze without alarm
browsing the tall grass in the derelict grounds up
the Arlington
in gauzy moonlight

Suspension

Big white nearly
full moon
with pouty cheek
rising above
cold November dream

Storm Light, from Ocean View

The big storm looms off shore in black ecstatic light
Preparing us for the violence of landfall
The old weird light of the North Pacific, cold

And deep, bright and dark
The blue wind in the thin black trees
And the pavement in the city street hissing

In the rain so late yet so strong in coming
Making up for a whole season strangely missing
As if until now it had had better things to do

Bridge

The stones rising from
           the gray
                       water

The dark bay, illegible
                    sentence
punctuated
by pier stumps — stubbed
matchsticks
broken piers jutting toward
                   emptiness

fishing nets
fresh snow on dark piers
converging in distance
loneliness cold winter
                  night

streaming weeds
               a blur
just beneath the surface

light is life

color joy

but now — all dark

and from those loved, drifting

poles
        apart
unready to cross
                over

a bridge between worlds

One Moment

One moment
One fortieth of a second
closer

Exposed

covering over
all the color
in the world
with white
and gray
but for a little
yellow patch
exposed tissue
where a limb
has torn
away and left
tender life
vulnerable
and open
to the cold

Ladybug

The ladybug I clumsily tried to rescue
But crushed under the window sill today
Isn't going to get over it

Did I suppose
Upon this well meant intervention
It would gratefully fly off homeward

Strange reward
Beautiful things ought to be left alone
In a natural state

Wild

A spiky
aromatic
fragrance, a bravery

Your light, which has always shown
brightest against
the darkness around it

Light Relief

Her laughter that rang out like a spoon struck upon a plate
hung in the air, and all the phones in that lost world went dead at
  once
the wind blew husklike clouds across an amber moon

                                        the years

if only, for an instant...

Fissure

Sounds of old timbers weeping in the dark
house in the cold night
for what is bent and broken —
a valued life —
and will never again be whole
even when the wind stops blowing

Things bend, break, fall apart. It's a mistake
to get in the way
of a force of nature. Confine it
here, it will pop up again
over there
when you're not looking.

And yes things have a way of changing,
when the wind stops blowing
there may yet come a time
in this world of the few
watchers and the many watched
when they've stopped looking.

Hidden Villa

fallen down hutch
dry rot
        broken step
leaf mulch
          detritus

litter village
     tangled
   under woods

      let there
         hang this
singular epithet
in the speech balloon:

      [—]*

———

* an imprecation heard
in weedy language

Christmas Market

Escape
forgot, numb
fingers
in half
gloves at
the bus stop
busy night
market holiday
shoppers with groaning
carts
rushing out
automatic door
to celebrate
what bus
an hour late
again

Diminishing Perspective

Everything that once seemed near
now seems far away. On the 18, Carlos
with bandaged hand
politely tucks his 12 ounce
can into the black plastic bag
which he switches into his rucksack
and says, Got to get indoors
soon. The rain the cold. I think
I'll get off at Cedar. No
maybe Vine.

Carlos
is in his sixties,
street grizzled,
a thinker
beyond his present
inconvenienced
station, holds
a post
graduate degree
in Roman history,

one year around this season
on the pavement outside
the chain pharmacy outlet
where Christmas trees were being sold
we discussed
the Star in the East,
the Journey of the Mages,
and Mazdaism,
with a military vet
in a baseball cap

who was pissed off
beyond apparent cause
or reason
until calmed by
thoughtful words — philosophy
a consolation
but this year
seems like
nobody's much
up for it.

Bait

Long shadows cast by distant dying sun fall
Downhill

People living half
in and half out of
total abandonment

The time Safeway's freezer failed
and all the perishables
ended up in the dumpster
at once

is still spoken of as a historic day
but tonight
with that hard northeast wind biting again
on the streets
nobody would want
a half melted Sara Lee frozen apple pie

Lunch Poem

That green plastic fish in the pool
made by the rocks along the trail in Tilden
offered the typical post romantic false
getaway into the natural, perhaps
but that was then and this is a different
time, the time of no way out, too late now

This town totally ate me for lunch
but not before keeping my brain packed up
in that swell green lunch box
for all those many months that turned
into all those many years of afterlife alas
not quite imperceptibly it must be admitted

It's a long time ago already now but oh my
I don't really know why unless it's the brain compression
the memory of that green plastic fish
or it may have been one of its several long forgot plastic rock
pool fish of many colors of yesteryear antecedents
lingers because
encounters of that sort always gave birth in me even then to

an insane wish to escape into the sky

Balancing

Your cane serves as a lever that allows you to stand up on the bus
You hobble a few steps down the aisle
Embarrassed
Swaying
Grasping the seat backs
The overhead strap
Unsteady
I wrote a letter to my love and on the way I dropped it
One of you has picked it up and put it in your pocket
It's not you, it's not you, it's not you...
Someone taps you on the back
It's your stop
You lurch toward the exit
Unsteady
Start to slip
And at the last moment catch yourself before falling

Stretching It

When you are having a philosophical conversation with someone and they are not able to think outside the box... you'd like to encourage them to think about it.

He's rounding second. Time slows down. Everything seems so far away. The image on the screen is frozen.

"Stretch it out!"

"A face only covers a skull awhile, so stretch that skull cover and smile!"

"Get two!"

This is by some called, the ghost of wit, delighting to ambulate after the death of its body.

And to say the truth, there seems to be no part of knowledge in fewer hands, than that of discerning when to have done.

A stretch. That's what it was always going to be.

"It's only the sixth. Why are you standing up?"

"All those other guys are doing it."

There were no promises. Things would happen as they happened.

I never expected to get thrown out at third.

By the way, have I told you? I am trying an experiment very frequent among recent authors, which is to write upon nothing, and when the subject is utterly exhausted, to let the pen, locked within the withered, knobbly digits, still move on, leaving its litter of semi-legible marks scattered across the virgin snows of the notebook page.

I didn't lie, either, I was only stretching the truth. I didn't know the guy had a gun for an arm.

Vulnerable

The non human
stares back across the final
                              abyss
at you, suburban
                    youth
in thin miserable late October neon night mist
entering the Spirit Halloween outlet
on Shattuck
to buy stinking Chinese plastic
fright mask, chimerical
                              simulacrum

which bares
the hapless fear
of the violated
                    in constraint

skyfalling

wild skyfalling night
tail of first big storm front of the season slashing through
last loose leaf debris hurried along
"as before an enchanter fleeing"
branches clattering against metal
trash cans banging around
all that's not securely fastened
caught up and blowing — apprehensive
electricity in the streets, guy wobbling little progress
on toppling bike against the gale
sidewalk woman head down moving slowly uphill
into northeast wind grabbing at swirling blown ends
of long diaphanous pastel scarf
Ninth and Bancroft, West Berkeley
insecure householder half dressed
emerges from behind barred gate
looks up into dark sky
one arm bent over head as if to shield, crouching —

Other

Dark shapes bundled
against the weather
separate, each an other
body
world closed
upon itself
no one looks up
masked passers-by
slowly
moving, known only
to the night and the cold

State of Emergency

as if the colored bulbs
strung upon
last year's discarded
Christmas tree
lit up miraculously
in the city
dump
in black and white
and shades of gray

Woman in the Window

The ghostly Madonna in the thriftshop window looked down
  at us
in compassion and with sorrow through shattered glass
without seeing us

from which wrecked perspective ships had been launched
while Joseph was off in the shed puttering
with those damned tools of his again

The View from Here

A strong jolt, the sound of heavy metal
and heavy metal interacting. Honk!
One of those long trains of white cloud
streaming onshore over El Cerrito
paused. The first driver pulled himself out.
Fat guy in khaki t-shirt. He said quietly, *Fuck.*
Standing at the window I turned away.

A Door in the Wall

Who's looking out?

Who's out there
looking in from the road
on which the world is passing by,

always growing larger
stranger and richer
or poorer and less strange

or older and narrower
in the rearview, as you
catch yourself looking

always away, off to
one side?

Why Me

Why me?
I asked.

I hadn't ever requested that.
Easter came and went.

The negative thoughts passed
and were replaced

by fresh negative thoughts
popping up

much as blossoms, to mark
the season

of renewal.

.

Two weeks went by
but little changed. The rain

ended, the city
deer grew thirsty

again. A Saturday
morning, broad daylight, traffic

mayhem as ever
on Marin. Then I saw her.

A bold doe
with fawns in tow

anxiously prancing
across Colusa

in the middle of the lethal
vehicular stream

at the corner where
the Jetta whacked me.

A few hours later
she was back on her own

standing on hind legs
pushing with front

on a sapling
so that it bent low

enough for nibbling.

Lust for Life

In life
even the emptiest day has something in it
whereas after life
even the fullest of days has
nothing in it
becomes a sort of mantra
after a while
as the empty days and nights
go by   wa-hoo!   yee-haw!

Lacuna

He stopped going out
stopping in was the final mistake,
the stairs too steep

Retreated to a nulliverse
where, dwelling within
the oneirotaxia of
an out of focus twilight
and watching the flags ripple
imperceptibly
in the faint breeze that played
through the rafters of the Arnett YMCA
on the lit up screen
above the organ,
he spent his last days

Opaque

Toy ships or pilot fish are floating memories.
And then, as the nonthreatening prerecorded sounds
drift down the aisle, and echoes of answering machine messages
meant for lost children eerily burble up
through the opaque blue glass museum display case
water, it starts to seem ok, a plastic chair waits for you,
having escaped the rocks of Kitchen Appliances,
to sink in and make yourself at home.

So Now You Know

It's been uphill all the way
you can't blow your own sail
but you can still blow your own horn
so long as no one's around to hear it

you can blow your lid
you can blow your wig
you can blow your top
you can blow your brains out

you can blow your cover
you can blow your cork
you can blow your lines
you can blow your one big shot

you can blow your nose
you can blow your whistle
you can blow your fuse
you can blow your cool
or maybe not
so now you know

Bright Ideas

the failing organism
impatiently
to the construct personality:
"You and your bright ideas
on fire
in that bag over your head again."

Blank (Don't Be Late)

A generation
mesmerized by
small screens

will always have
its own image
to remember itself

by

Millennial Rising

When we reach the threshold of our aspirations
We know that the uplifting beam of generational self approval
  will fall over us
Slip quietly beneath us without our really knowing it
And transport us as if by magic carpet
Into a challenging yet inspiring new dimension in which
We will take on the amazing ability to stand upright under our
  own power
And reach up with fingertips at least partially extended
And maybe even almost touch the ceiling
So as to change the world

Rue (Melancholy Couple)

It hadn't always been this way.
A hundred years ago things had been
Well, in a certain way... clearer, simpler.
That was before mother had come to stay.
She had been able to sit up straight then
And to at least put up an appearance of civility.
He had been able to actually *read*
His book, rather than merely to pretend rigidly
To be holding it. Neither understood
The viselike dominion of necessity in which
Their lives were gripped. For this
Melancholy couple things would remain
This way forever. Gaze
Upon them, and learn from their story.

The Beginning

Every morning bright and early
Came the man with the channels
Then one day he did not come
That was the day the dust storms began
Don't blame it on the cable guy

Doom Forest

somewhere in the cartoon suspended
animation silence of the exurban commuter night
quietly behind a stageprop gated wall
rain falls softly on the cell phone tower trees

Party Animals

The party animals all lay battered
and discarded
in the weeds and tall grass
with the party long since over

a lot of time would have to pass
with no one to notice it
before the march of progress
could begin again

Peerage

A time to embrace, a time
to refrain

from embracing
one's own reflection

in the wetspot
in the parkinglot

of the Mini Mart
when the party's over

Still Lights

On the seventh day
He rested.

For eons
He had waited

Until the time was right
To lure

Big tech firms
Into the cleanest

Little white
City

He had ever
Created.

And then, and then
Into the silence

He shone
His lights —

His red light
His green light

And his computer
Timed don't

Walk signal.

Negative Development

Death avoidance.
A game like tag.
An everyday thing.

Haben einen schönen Tag.
Haben einen schönen Tod.

Old is a kind of plague.

The demented chef
could not remember her own recipe
between looking it up
and turning around
thus ruining the duck
she was cooking for the food editor.

At that point she threw in the apron
and went to the superfood
and microvitamin
cocktails.

Always the broken door
swinging on its hinges
in the ancient gate,
the rue in the not knowing
whether or not
the imperial warriors are out there
or
the dosage intakes
actually occurred
as prescribed.

And the sympathy
felt for the duck —
where, along the smoothie
greased path
leading to the next dim covert
in life's incredible journey
was there ever going to be
time for that?

Not Wading But Sinking

That sinking feeling
The business lunch
Heavy on the lap —
Small knoblike men
Gripping power briefcases —
Inertia of the social mass
Lapped by fetid waters —
Wading amid toxin
Saturated weeds —
Zombified — floating sacs —
Playdough bodies —
Moving in lemming packs
Through dead cities
Toward inevitable collapse

Product Placement

As the rip in the screen
the tear in the curtain
the edge of the frame
permits you to see
once again
through the fabrication
to the reality
the window that opens
upon the greater deception
hidden
at the bottom of the bin

Emotional

Emotional
distance between viewer
and screen growing
ever greater, the coldness
of the space
intervening ever deeper,
the mourning
all that's lost
more remote
and diluted
with each minute
and second
that goes by

Sheepish

Tentative, hanging back
hesitant
to speak — in a world

endlessly fraught
with administrative
penalties

for those tempted
to utter
so much as one

independent word
in the face of
the expanding

control
mechanisms,
tending

to one's knitting
in public
makes one sheepish,

stitched up,
stuck in, half afraid
to risk a peek

at what might
or might not
be waiting out

there.

Express

It's being put about
there's a secret vault
beneath the lifetime care unit

What got lost in the cracks
when "we" didn't quite
come together

"as a people"
must be down
there somewhere

Imaging (The White Horse)

The white horse parked in your ghost corral is going nowhere,
soldier. And from the front line, the imaging
center, the fear factory, these reports: sounding a well

of sorrow deeper than the deepest ocean. Always an asymmetric
warfare: freefalling
through an area of phantom density, lucency, shadowchasing

behind lead shields. "They give out numbers. You are put in
  a room
where all the numbers
are waiting to go inside the tubes. And no one's saying a word."
  Eight

worried women naked
under blue hospital kimonos, waiting in silence
not for any imaginable compassion

but for the computer
malfunction
to end.

Fear

Not that being one of them
ever softened the view
                    but pain
makes it clearer
the fear
seen in their eyes
as they inflict suffering
upon something living, well
it's natural —
it's plain
it's clear

that they have cause
they have reason
to be afraid

I Am Alive (Bounded by Forest)

The suffering, now
unceasing. The sense of violation
passive and in the face
of extraction, unresisting
as can be seen in this general view.
They came and cut out the parts
they wanted, and took them away.
What remained was changed
forever, as a waste of shame
lost in its own autism,
last refuge of the victim without
a name.

Interrogation

You always have to know the right question
The one to which there can never be a correct reply

Lionize

If a lion could talk, we could not understand him.
—Ludwig Wittgenstein: *Philosophical Investigations*

If a lion could talk,
   would he talk to Mark
   would he talk to Matthew
   would he talk to Luke
   would he talk to John

or to the four archangels
mounted on the queen's bedposts

No

even if he were in great pain
even if his life were ending
even if the hyena pack were closing in
and the vultures already wheeling in patient circles
in a wide early evening sky
he would not let on

and we would continue to fail to understand him

Who goes there?

A movement
Something on the air

a half
mile off

in the bush —
an intruder?

Never not
on the alert —

Who goes there? —
startled to flight

the ever vigilant
dik-dik bolts

at the merest
hint

of the presence
of you

Something

Is it the light?

Something. Escaping the enclosure
somehow, slipping under
and heading off somewhere

or other. How far
How high how deep
won't matter

just go.

Then and Now

Then it was always
for now, later
for later.
And then years of now
passed, and it grew later
and later. Trapped
in the shrinking
chocolate box
the confused sardine
was unhappy. It
leapt, and banged its head
again. And afterward
they said shall we
repeat the experiment.
And it said
later for that.

America (Razor Sharp Cuts)

As the shades of evening come down
The colour of the spattermarks seems to be changing
From golden autumnal red to a deep rich brown
Tone of old mahogany or teak.

Blood matures as it dries.
By tomorrow they'll have hosed
The telltale stains off the pavement, by next week
No one will remember what happened,

Still the next act of the dark farce will never be far to seek,
A tableau vivant
Waiting behind the billowing black curtain
Hung above the neon lit stage

That's actually a vacant lot
Rank with last summer's tall weeds
Behind a taller security fence:
The place known as America,

All anyone could ever want,
And hidden somewhere in its aching blue night
There will always be the longshot hope for a new morning
Until there's not.

Recovered Memory

We landed successfully on the alien planet
but after conducting required observations
determined conditions were negative
for exiting the containing membrane
and then day followed night once again —
ice formed inside the great glass paperweight
as it lifted off into the cold black sky.

Appointment

the outlook always
unclear

the purpose forever
shrouded

the shadow of a body
in the trampled grass

Myth

Some out of fashion goddesses and gods
made clay replicas of themselves
and called them their children
and threw them into the fire
then went away
and when they came back later
it seemed the curse had been lifted
for it was quiet throughout the village
apart from the familiar sounds
of the traditional work continuing on

After the Flood

Into ripples fanning
circles in the freshet

that lapped
the field of flowers

that bathed
the white horse

after the flood
light poured

Giuseppe Ungaretti: Sunset

The sky's chaste flesh
awakens oases
in the nomad of love

Giuseppe Ungaretti: In Memoria

Locvizza 30 September 1916

His name was
Mohamed Sceab

Descendant
of emirs of nomadic tribes
took his own life
because he had lost
his homeland

Loved France
and changed his name

Was Marcel
but wasn't French
had forgot how
to simply live
sipping a coffee
in the tent of his people
where the little singsong
of the Koran is chanted

And didn't know how to
give
his separateness
a voice

I went along with the concierge
from the hotel where we lived
in Paris
following his body
down the dingy alleyway
from number 5 rue des Carmes

His remains
rest
in the cemetery at Ivry
dolorous suburb
that always brings to mind
the day
a fairground comes down

It may be I alone
still know
he was once alive

Impending: Hölderlin's Brevity

"Why so brief these days? Don't your songs move you
    as they once did? Back when you were young
        and your days were full of hope and you wanted
            Your singing never to come to an end?"

As my luck goes, so goes my song. Would you have the glow
    of the setting sun put you right? It's gone! Earth grows cold
        and the ungainly bird of night flutters down
            much too near, so that you must shield your eyes.

Dust Devil Days

To feel, then not
to feel
the swirl

Here, there, everywhere

Life in the lithosphere

Dust devil days
at the derelict oasis
Wind kicks up

A blur off in the distance
animation imperfect
resolution vagrant
wandering late
who? awaits what
outcome?

Blown Away

ephemeral as tinkerbell
unmoored yet not unmoved
tossed cloudward, flipped
       sans volition
into the flow

going but not wanting to go
without the other flotsam

Tom Clark was born in Chicago in 1941 and educated at the University of Michigan, Cambridge University and the University of Essex. He has worked variously as an editor (*The Paris Review*), critic (*Los Angeles Times, San Francisco Chronicle*) and biographer (lives of Damon Runyon, Jack Kerouac, Charles Olson, Robert Creeley, Edward Dorn), has published novels (*Who is Sylvia?, The Exile of Céline, The Spell*), memoirs (*Jim Carroll, Late Returns: A Memoir of Ted Berrigan*) and essays (*The Poetry Beat, Problems of Thought: Paradoxical Essays*). His many collections of poetry have included *Stones, Air, At Malibu, John's Heart, When Things Get Tough on Easy Street, Paradise Resisted, Disordered Ideas, Fractured Karma, Sleepwalker's Fate, Junkets on a Sad Planet: Scenes from the Life of John Keats, Like Real People, Empire of Skin, Light and Shade, The New World, Something in the Air, Feeling for the Ground, At the Fair, Canyonesque, Distance* and *Truth Game*. He lives in Berkeley, California with his wife and partner of forty-six years, Angelica Heinegg.

97302160R00061

Made in the USA
Middletown, DE
04 November 2018